NETS OF WONDER

Nets of Wonder

Olive Travers

Illustrations by Barry Britton
Music by Eamon Travers

BEEHIVE

Published 2023 by
Beehive Books
7–8 Lower Abbey Street
Dublin 1, Ireland
publications@veritas.ie
www.veritas.ie

ISBN 978-1-80097-058-8

Beehive Books is an imprint of Veritas Publications.

The following pieces were first broadcast on *Sunday Miscellany*, RTÉ Radio 1, and are reproduced here by kind permission of RTÉ: 'A Baby for All Seasons', 'Valentine's Bells', 'Dear Sean', 'Tea in the Hayfield', 'Back to the Fuchsia', 'Mass Cat, Mascot', 'For Fear of Little Men', 'Train Stations and Mothers with Sons', 'Remembering the Dead', 'The Gifted Life' and 'Auntie Gretta'.

Lines by T.S. Eliot on p. 15 from 'Burnt Norton', *Four Quartets*, London: Faber and Faber Ltd. Used with permission; lines by Francis Harvey on p. 32 from *Donegal Haiku*, Dublin: Dedalus Press, 2013. Used by kind permission of Dedalus Press, www.dedaluspress.com; lines by William Allingham on pp. 45–9 from 'The Fairies', 1850; lines by W.B. Yeats on p. 43 from 'The Cat and the Moon', 1919, and on p. 47 from 'The Stolen Child', 1889; lines by Emily Dickinson on p. 62 from 'Drowning is not so pitiful', 1718.

10 9 8 7 6 5 4 3 2 1

A catalogue record for this book is available from the British Library.

Designed by Lir Mac Cárthaigh
Printed in Northern Ireland by W&G Baird Ltd, Antrim

Beehive Books is a member of Publishing Ireland.

Beehive books are printed on paper made from the wood pulp of managed forests. For every tree felled, at least one tree is planted, thereby renewing natural resources.

Contents ❧

Introduction ❧

Nets of Wonder is a creative collaboration between Olive, a writer, Barry, an artist, and Eamon, a musician, spearheaded and inspired by Olive's writings. It began, as many good ideas do, around a kitchen table. In this instance it was Olive's kitchen table, where she gave her good friend Barry a sheaf of her writing, comprised mainly of scripts for RTÉ Radio 1's *Sunday Miscellany*. Barry chose twelve pieces that sparked his creativity and for each he illustrated a response. Olive's son Eamon took those same twelve scripts and composed an original piece of music to reflect the mood and theme of each.

In this selection of writing Olive, who is also a clinical psychologist, shifts her psychological lens away from others to mine her own memories, relationships and experiences. The resulting reflections are by turns fascinating, touching, funny and intensely sad, but always insightful. They celebrate not only great events but also those ordinary events that shine out from or cast a shadow over everyday life.

It is often said that there is no alternative to the feel of a book, the reassuring weight and welcoming warmth of paper in your hands. In this book, where each piece of writing has its own themed artwork and musical response, you are free to choose your own sensory experience. You can read Olive's pieces with Eamon's themed musical compositions playing in the background, using Barry's enchanting illustrations as a place to rest your eyes during contemplative pauses. You can listen through the album of Eamon's evocative music with eyes firmly fixed on the respective artworks, then re-explore those moods through the lens of Olive's words. Indeed, you could enter into the world within worlds contained in Barry's magical illustrations before returning to Olive's musings or to listen to a tune from Eamon.

You are invited to become a collaborator in this creative work, to unpack and unfurl these pieces according to your mood, to find your own unique path to entanglement in these nets of wonder.

Nets of Wonder by Eamon Travers ❦

Each story in *Nets of Wonder* has an accompanying piece of original music. You can listen to the album by scanning the QR code below.

TRACKLIST
A Baby for All Seasons
Valentine's Bells
Dear Sean
Tea in the Hayfield
Back to the Fuchsia
The Big Tent
Mass Cat, Mascot
For Fear of Little Men
Train Stations and Mothers with Sons
Remembering the Dead
The Gifted Life
Auntie Gretta

SPRING

A Baby for All Seasons ✻

he year has tipped, the sun is inching its way up the sky and lengthening rays hold the promise of a still-distant spring. I walk the narrow coast road to visit my newborn grandson, through a world honed back to its essentials. Sunshine, cleansed by earlier rain, makes raindrops glisten on the skeletons of fuchsia in wind-flayed fields. The Atlantic stretched out on the horizon is flooded with transparent winter light. A tiny wren jinks between the stones of the dry-stone wall, uttering a few high, clear notes. The air is cool and fresh but indoors is cosy with the fizzing stove wrapping warmth around me. The sleeping presence of the new baby fills the house. My daughter takes advantage of the burst of sunshine to walk the short distance to the pier, separating for the first time from her baby after nine months of being one. Being alone with this new life suddenly awes me. He lies in a straw Moses basket, one arm stretched above his head, his face in profile with soft, downy hair covering his fragile skull and the pulse of his heartbeat in the open gap of his fontanelle. He is sleeping but not still – he makes a sucking motion with his tiny mouth and utters little beads of sound. His eyelids are transparent and blue-veined. Everything about him is heart-stopping and utterly perfect; how small all our lives are in the beginning, how big they become with our hopes and dreams and how small again at the end. Anthropologist Mary Catherine Bateson sees all our lives as a single, interconnected whole: she believes that the idea of an individual, the idea that there is someone to be known separate from the relationship, is an error. She insists that we create each other, bring each other into being by being part of the matrix in which the other exists.

It is amazing how this tiny new life commands the attention and love of so many people. In the months of anticipation in this high-tech world of diminishing mystery, he was the ultimate mystery, with his parents choosing not to know if the baby coming to meet them was a boy or a girl. Now, in the year ahead, the growth of this tiny seed of a person will mark the seasons spooling through the first year of his life – the translucent light of spring, the thrumming fullness of summer, the subdued grandeur of autumn and the silvery darkness of winter. With him, we push our quivering hearts bravely into the unknown year and the unknown future. He represents that timeless projection of all our hopes at the start of each year, that with each new beginning we can figure out our place in the flow of time, and believe that our lives have not been lived for nothing. My thoughts are interrupted as the baby arches his back and gives a sharp, splintery little cry. Having been alerted to the possibility of wind, I tentatively cup his head in my hand and, with my other hand under his back, lift him against my chest. He moulds into me in a way that is achingly familiar. He may be fragile as glass but he is atremble with an inner energy and I can feel the flurry of his breath in his ribcage. The forward rush of my own life is crystallised into this golden moment as a shaft of winter sun comes through the window, turning the room to honey. This is T.S. Eliot's 'still point of the turning world':

At the still point of the turning world. Neither flesh
　　nor fleshless;
Neither from nor towards; at the still point, there
　　the dance is ...

This is what I remember from when my children were babies: life honed down, elemental. It loses its complexities – the angst of too many choices, too many decisions.

When my daughter returns, she, with that exquisite radar of the new mother, makes a beeline for her baby before she even takes off her coat. The entire room inhales the clear, cold salt air she brings in with her. It is time for me to leave this haven, where, softly in the sky-blues of baby cards and brightly in the bouquets of flowers, happiness has invaded.

Valentine's Bells ✤

It is Saturday, 14 February 1970. The girl is fifteen; the boy is sixteen. The girl lives four miles out of town and the only time she can meet the boy in the town is on Saturday afternoons while her parents are doing their weekly shopping. Each week her heart lurches in anticipation when the church, with its clock tower perched high above the hilly town, comes into view. She is almost there. On this special day she feels as if her heart is bobbing on a piece of elastic when she sees the boy waiting for her. They exchange cards. He gives her a sumptuous one with a satin heart and roses. It plays the theme song from the film *Love Story* when she opens it. Its first line is perfect: 'Where do I begin to tell the story of how great a love can be?'

The girl feels the bewildering, happy sense of being able to touch someone else's heart. It is a pet day, the sky the clear blue-green of a thrush's egg. The girl and the boy walk hand in hand up the steep hill of the town's main street, then up a narrow side street that ends at the gates of the church. Books and poems and dreams are buzzing around like bees in the girl's head. She wants to see the grave of the poet William Allingham. The church warden brings them to it.

Then he tells them that the church clock has just had a spring clean. The girl goes into the church, where she hears something stir in the heart of its shadowy stillness. The door to the clock tower is open. She climbs the steep, smooth stone steps, which bring her right into the face of the clock. The scale is so huge the girl feels like one of Gulliver's Lilliputians. Below her the slowly turning cogs and wheels control the forward rush of time with their disciplined click and clack. Beside her the huge clock hands quiver and tremble in anticipation of their next move. Then, the mechanism below whirrs, the giant hands click as if surprised, and the dong of the quarter-hour chime explodes in the tower. The girl feels all her senses vibrate at full pitch long after the sound has flown downhill over the town, and out to the sea beyond.

To her astonishment the thought comes that she will one day die. She feels, for the first time in her life, that she is fully alive and that everything is alive along with her. Even the poet and all the other dead under their tombstones in the graveyard below would once have heard this clock chime as she does now, and they hold the same memory of happiness in their bones. She feels intensely happy in a boundless world full of possibilities. She also feels for the first time that she is happy to be in the present instead of always on the way to elsewhere, always pressing into the future. Outside, everything gleams cleanly in the soft spring sunshine, and the boy is waiting.

Many years have passed since I was that girl on that Valentine's Day. At times, my innermost heart still feels like that of the fifteen-year-old girl in spite of the message the mirror gives me that time has evaporated like the dew. I still have that Valentine's card. Its rusted music box no longer chimes out the question, 'Where do I begin to tell the story of how great a love can be?' It does not need to. The man that sixteen-year-old boy became is still by my side and the chimes of the quarters, halves and hours of our years together have been measured by the chiming of that same church clock. It looks benignly down at me when I look out the kitchen window of our home. It has witnessed our four children growing up and moving into their own worlds of possibilities. Now it sees that girl and boy on their own again.

The story is still unfolding.

Dear Sean ❧

y mother, who died in 2006, was a hoarder. Among the eighty years of memorabilia she had squirrelled away in an attic was a 1966 *Irish Press* supplement commemorating the fiftieth anniversary of the 1916 Rising. The fact that she kept it was not in keeping with her as she had loved all things royal and never missed the Queen's Christmas speech. London, where she had trained as a nurse in the 1940s, was her El Dorado. It represented the glamorous unlived life she had exchanged for one tethered by seven children to a small farm in Fermanagh.

When her house was cleared the supplement went into another attic and remained undisturbed until 2016 when it was resurrected for the year that was in it. Only then did it give up its purpose. Out of it fell a letter to my then ten-year-old brother Sean, which my mother had written on the evening of Easter Sunday, 1966.

'Dear Sean,' she writes, 'This is a historic day. I wonder where you will be in fifty years' time and what changes there will be, for changes are inevitable.' She tells him what he did on the day, how we all went to Mass, and she lists the litany of our seven names and ages: Valentia, Maureen, Olive, Sean, Gerald, James and Julie. There is special mention of how Julie, the three-year-old youngest, is 'such a pretty little girl with her ringlets'. She tells him that he had a roast chicken dinner, peach trifle for sweet and in the evening a picnic on Mushroom Hill where Dada lit a fire. She writes, 'You all had great fun. You are young, healthy and happy.'

Fifty years on, in July 2016, as I stand at a reopened grave, my living memory allows me to put flesh on the bones of her words. Behind her pride in her baby's ringlets is my picture of her patience in mummifying strands of hair by wrapping each around and around in long strings of cloth and knotting each one at the end to create spring-sprung curls you could put your finger into.

'We all went to Mass' is shorthand for seven children packed into the back seat and boot of my father's battered boxy Hillman Hunter – aptly nicknamed 'The Biscuit Box' for its dusky pink colour. As for 'roast chicken dinner', so much carnage contained in so few words: how an unsuspecting high-stepping hen became a flurry of outraged flapping wings as my mother deftly wrung its neck and yanked the feathers from its still-warm body. Peach trifle was a calmer affair – a delightful concoction of sponge fingers and tinned peaches, soaked in Chivers red jelly and topped with Bird's custard powder. Picnics, my mother's way of marking special occasions, were real treats in spite of the fact that Mushroom Hill was only two fields away from the house. Dada, still in his good Mass clothes, took charge of us gathering sticks to make a fire in which, on that Easter Sunday, eggs would have ceremoniously boiled in the water that was then used to make tea.

There are so many happy memories for me in the dead piece of paper of my mother's letter. While the newspaper she placed it in commemorated a great event, her letter captures how there were jewels of days in her ordinary life. I like to imagine her as happy and fulfilled when she took the time to record that day for her much-loved and longed-for eldest son, who had arrived after three daughters. There were many more jewels, as well as her share of life's sorrows, in her remaining forty years. She was not to know as she wrote that letter that even as her son delighted in the surprise gift of it fifty years later, death was already lurking to take him without warning. As Sean's coffin was lowered into the same grave where she and my father are buried, the answer to her rhetorical question – I wonder where you will be in fifty years? – is that he is where she would have least wanted him to be.

SUMMER

Tea in the Hayfield ✺

here are more than one billion people in India and I feel as if they have all converged on me. I am unnerved by the death-defying experience of crossing the street in the city of Kozhikode. I have had to weave my way through the ballistic dance of buses, trucks, tuk-tuks, scooters and oxen carts. I take refuge in a street-side café and nab a seat under the welcoming cool of a ceaselessly revolving ceiling fan. Nothing is familiar. All around me is a riot of strange colours, sounds and smells. It is as if I have accidentally wandered onto the stage during some lively drama involving characters in flowing robes, saris, burqas and turbans.

Then, unbidden, a thick glass of milky tea appears in front of me. I sip it. It is smoke-flavoured, very hot, very strong and very sweet. As I drink it my Auntie Gretta comes surging through half a century of time and several continents into the café.

I am a child again on my summer holidays in my grandmother's childless house on the shores of Lough Erne, where Gretta reigns over the kitchen. My grandmother is there but somewhere at the edges, all black and lean and angles. It is Gretta who takes charge of bringing tea to the men in the hayfield and no temple acolyte feels more important than I do in my role as her chief helper. Gretta seems to be always doing. A gossamer blanket of flour dust coats the navy, rose-sprigged wrap-around pinny covering her ample frame as she kneads the soda bread. The dough springs back as she presses her knuckles into it. It is my job then to cut a deep cross in it before she puts it into the pot oven on the open-hearth fire. Her wiry, unruly hair escapes from its clips and flops around her horn-rimmed glasses as she piles hot coals on the oven lid with long black tongs. She drops the kettle down three notches and swings the crook over the flames. Soon she is wetting and brewing and sugaring the golden-brown tea and pouring it into miniature metal milk churns.

I help with the buttering of thick wedges of warm soda bread, the wrapping of it in cloths and the filling of an empty HP sauce bottle with milk from the cool flagged dairy. Everything is packed into two large wicker baskets. I follow Gretta and she leads me through a maze map of fields, each one opening into the next through hidden gaps in hawthorn hedges fringed with creamy honeysuckle, meadowsweet and yarrow. The sound of cattle cudding in the shade of the hedges duets with Gretta puffing and panting, her arms dragged down by the baskets.

At last we reach the hayfield. There, three big loose-limbed men choreograph a precise hay dance: one rakes in the hay, another pitches it onto the ruck and the third, high up on the ruck, tramples it down. It is as if some hay god is pulling the strings of puppets in perfect synchronicity: rake, pitch, trample; rake, pitch, trample.

The dance comes slowly to a halt and sun-reddened faces dissolve into smiles of welcome. There is little talking done until the last drop of tea has been drained from the can. With backs resting against the ruck, arms burnt brown to the elbow make expeditions into deep pockets and pull out cigarettes. Then I hear a foretelling of how, through the G8 summit, this same Lough Erne would one day give its name to communiqués and declarations to the world. Between contented sighs and the exhaling of smoke, proclamations of 'I declare to God', ''tis a holy terror', and 'it's a quare turnabout' wash over me as the men dissect the politics of the parish.

The hayfield and Lough Erne below it give way to the thicket of Indian traffic and the steamy activity of the café but the tea remains. As I sip it I begin to look beyond the strangeness of my surroundings and see that even in the polyglot confusion of this unfamiliar culture, tea and chat remain a constant. I drain my glass and signal to one of the scurry of waiters for a refill.

Back to the Fuchsia

n our rugged north-west coast the profusion of fragile flowers of the fuchsia is an enigma. My appreciation now of its beauty is based on the truism that you only really miss something when it's gone. All my life I took for granted that from early summer into early winter it would just be there – its slender, arching, flower-laden branches striving to hold hands over winding grassy back roads. Then some years ago, the unthinkable happened. After an unprecedented big winter freeze, while other plants eventually sprouted green to announce spring, the fuchsia continued to wear its toffee-coloured winter coat. I had almost given up hope when at last soft, new growth sprouted tentatively from its base. My delight now in its return to full health is in proportion to the loss I felt when I thought we had lost it forever. Their fragility is deceptive. Fuchsia thrives on our wind-scarred, rocky coasts, flaunting its beauty against the backdrop of the constant flux of sea light. It is a beauty as variable as our weather, rain sweeping in veils over it makes the hedges throb and pulse with its blood-red and purple flowers, leading to its name in Irish, *Deora Dé*, the Tears of God. When the sun and sea breezes caress it, its bell-shaped flowers are long-legged ballerinas pirouetting in their purple and crimson tutus. Long before we were repackaged as the Wild Atlantic Way, its colours would have echoed the traditional red and mauve petticoats worn by western-seaboard women. Now, like some trendy avant-garde gardener, it thumbs its nose at conventional colour combinations and chooses as its roadside companion the blazing orange spires of montbretias.

We take the omnipresence of fuchsia so for granted it is hard to believe that it is not a native; in fact, its bright colours were designed by nature to attract the hummingbirds in its home near the Magellan straits in Chile. Its origins are in its botanical name – *Fuchsia magellanica*. As children, we called it honeysuckle as, like the hummingbird, we perfected the art of sucking out the sweet pouch of nectar from its flower base; this involved removing the petals and squeezing the pouch straight into our mouths – a pleasure that left us with ghoulish red- and purple-stained lips.

Its bell flowers are also called 'lady's eardrops'; a fact which Donegal poet Francis Harvey pithily turns into a haiku:

> She wants red earrings
> Poor me, I present her with
> two fuchsia blooms.

French monk and botanist Charles Plumier is credited with bringing it to this part of the world after he discovered it on a plant-finding trip to Chile in 1703. He named it after a renowned sixteenth-century German doctor and botanist called Leonhart Fuchs – little knowing that the good Doctor Fuchs would end up immortalised in the hedgerows of the west of Ireland. In later years, even eminent scientists like Charles Darwin were not immune to its charms in its natural habitat. In his *The Voyage of the Beagle*, written in the 1830s, Darwin describes how when climbing a mountain in Chile 'there were several extensive breaks of the fuchsia, covered with its very beautiful drooping flowers, but very difficult to crawl through'.

It was, unsurprisingly, a big hit with gardeners in the England of the eighteenth century – although George Eliot (Mary Anne Evans), in the 1860 novel *The Mill on the Floss*, notes that an elderberry bush is a 'more gladdening sight' than the finest fuchsia. Inevitably it made its way across the water and ended up in the gardens of the Big Houses in Ireland. Anyone who has stuck a fuchsia branch into the ground and seen how easily it grows limbs will understand how quickly it escaped from cultivated gardens and spread through dumped garden prunings. Its vigorous, fast-growing qualities meant it was soon planted deliberately as a hedging plant.

Charles Darwin would probably tell me that if fuchsia does disappear as a result of our colder winters, it will be as a result of evolution and natural selection. That would be little consolation, though, for the loss of this beautiful and exotic alien that we have taken to our hearts.

Ballyshannon
Music Festival
Traditional

1st 2nd 3rd
August 1986

- NA CASAIDIGH
- THE SANDS FAMILY
- ANDY IRVINE • FREDDIE WHITE
- LIAM OG Ó FLOINN • OISÍN
- CHARLIE McGETTIGAN/
ARTY McGLYNN/NOLLAIG CASEY
- PADDY GLACKEN AND DONAL LUNNY
- KIERAN GOSS • CURLEW • HERITAGE
- KIERAN HALPIN & MANUS LUNNY
- CRAN • JIM McCANN • CONAILLACH
- McSHERRY FAMILY • & MANY MORE
- WITH COMPERE TOMMY SANDS

WEEKEND TICKETS £15.00 •
FREE FULLY SERVICED CAMP SITES •
AFTERNOON CEILIDHE •
WORKSHOPS • STREET THEATRE •
SESSIONS COMMENCING
TUESDAY 29th JULY

© BARRY BRITTON DESIGN STUDIO, DONEGAL TOWN

The Big Tent

I want to take you back to the 1980s when the intoxicating smell of canvas and trampled grass marked the stepping out of clock time. On the August bank holiday weekend the huge canvas marquee known as the Tent, home of the Ballyshannon Folk Festival, arrived. Without internet, mobile phones and often not even a landline, the organisation of the festival is a huge task.

My other half, Anthony, is right in the heart of that work. Our postman is weighed down with bags of demo cassette tapes and the clunk and click of the cassette player is a constant in our house. The year 1980 sees the first of artist Barry Britton's now-iconic posters, the unveiling of which makes the much-anticipated final line-up a reality.

Soldiers from Finner Camp work shoulder to shoulder with local volunteers to get the tent up and it rises like a giant mushroom in the centre of the town. There is the heaving and holding taut of the heavy guy ropes to raise giant supporting poles and the hoisting upright of the flapping canvas top and side walls. Strong stakes are driven home into the ground to secure the structure and then the bass-drum hammering of the maple sprung-floor sections tattoos our anticipation aloud.

Spores of tents spread out from that giant mushroom and a tented village springs up on the local GAA grounds before overflowing onto every available green space in the town, including our garden. Our house becomes a microcosm of the cross-fertilisation of music and friendship happening all over the town with the annual reunion of many musicians and performers, while down the town crowds flow like multicoloured rivers through the narrow, hilly streets. They gather together in small knots or larger clusters around the street-music sessions, the street performers, the sizzling burger vans, the face-painting and the stalls selling tie-dye, batiks and all manner of gewgaws.

Above it all rises the chanting, drum beating and cymbal clashing of the orange-clad Hare Krishnas with their hypnotic chant, 'Hare Krishna, Hare Krishna, Krishna, Krishna, Hare Hare, Hare Rama, Hare Rama.'

The afternoon céilidhe in the Tent sees big, burly Germans making up for with enthusiasm what they lack in skill as they swing local dancers like dandelion down into the air and Pat McGee, the Fear an Tí, calls 'The Waves of Tory'.

Evening sees the earnest, music-loving continentals arrive early in the marquee to claim floor space in front of the stage for the concerts, which last anything from five to seven hours, depending on the mood of the performers. As the night progresses the local stewards have to engage in skilled diplomacy to equal that of Boutros Boutros-Ghali to avoid international incidents as the well-lubricated, out-for-the-craic brigade surge towards the stage for the main acts.

On balmy nights the sides of the marquee are rolled up, releasing waves of heat, sweat and cigarette smoke, and loops of music coil and uncoil up the sides of the natural amphitheatre of the town's hills, and when sheets of torrential rain belt the canvas it becomes a musical ark.

All the greats of the Irish folk and traditional music scene grace that stage. Christy Moore, spraying sweat, holding the audience in the palm of his hand with his Ballyshannon version of 'Lisdoonvarna', The Sands Family uniting the audience in a rousing anthem of 'Nicaragua, We hear you', Kieran Goss and the Woman's Heart phenomenon bringing the biggest crowd ever, and the sprung wooden floors vibrating as the music of De Danann, Altan, Dervish and a host of other wonderful performers thump into the body with an almost physical intensity.

Then on Monday it is all over, the hallucinatory spell is broken, the buses are packed and every road out of town lined with hitchhiking weary, sweaty bodies.

Those 1980s festivals are now dreamlike, topsy-turvy memories of that special kind of magic that comes with walking home at dawn after all-night music sessions before crawling into the delicious comfort of my bed with the sun spangling the edges of the curtains.

Over the forty-six years of its existence the festival has morphed to cater for those of us who could sit for hours on a wooden floor but who now know what Leonard Cohen meant when he sang about aching in the places where he used to play. We may now sit on soft seats instead of a wooden floor but that timeless alchemy of live music weaving lives together endures.

AUTUMN

Mass Cat, Mascot ✻

 n Sundays, before 11 o'clock Mass in Rossnowlagh, a ginger and white tomcat slips around the edge of the church door and pads sinuously down the aisle to the altar. With an athletic spring, he jumps up onto the red velvet cushion on a carved chair. From there he and the congregation can observe each other with mutual curiosity. The Franciscan Friars named this stray Thomas but he is best known as Mass Cat. For the next hour voices and song ripple over him and the smell of incense and candles thrill his nostrils. As the sun reaches the stained-glass windows above the altar it bathes him in a rainbow benediction of light. Sometimes he dozes, lying on his stomach, curling his tail up under him with one leg draped languidly over the edge of the chair. During the commotion of communion he sits up, rolls his large, calm, whiskered face around, yawns, licks his paws, and settles down again into his world of dreams.

Where better could this stray cat have found refuge than under the protection of St Francis, patron saint of animals? Outside the church is a full-sized statue of Francis surrounded by birds, and while there is no mention of a cat, there is a well-known story about the Saint befriending a wolf. It must be the Saint's influence that allows Mass Cat to be so at home among all these birds, rather than stalking them with murderous intent.

I wonder did some stirring of inherited memory of his ninth-century ancestor Pangur Bán bring this stray to the monastery. That cat is celebrated by another monk, in another time, working alone in his cell, who compares his work as a scholar with the activities of his cat.

> I and Pangur Bán my cat,
> 'Tis a like task we are at:
> Hunting mice is his delight,
> Hunting words I sit all night.

Or was it the memory of a thirteenth-century Franciscan monk Bartholomew, author of the nineteen volumes of *On the Properties of Things*, who provides a detailed description of cats including how the cat in youth is 'swift, pliant and merry, and leapeth and rusheth on everything that is before him' and, in age, a 'right heavy beast, full sleeping and lyeth slyly in wait for mice'.

Well, I don't know how old Mass Cat is, but when a sudden movement alarms him, with a predator's alertness, he crouches down in attack mode; however, there is a shortage of church mice in the Friary. Life was very different for a famous fourteenth-century cat. He belonged to Dame Julian of Norwich, who lived during a time when women who wrote were in danger of being burnt as heretics. During her monastic life as an anchorite, she had no contact with the world but did keep a cat to control the mice. This led to the popular image of her with a cat curled up at her feet as they together engaged with timeless questions about life, love and the meaning of suffering. Mother Julian's conclusion that 'All shall be well, all shall be well, and all manner of things shall be well' has endured through the centuries.

Indeed, Mass Cat is also partial to human ruminations and is a regular attendee at the annual Mícheál Ó Cléirigh Summer School based at the Friary. I have seen him compete successfully for attention with a learned speaker by shimmying up a dividing screen and, by carefully planting paw after paw on the narrow top, doing an acrobatic tightrope walk across it, casually stopping now and then to shake each paw.

It may have been the mutually beneficial arrangement of cats hunting the mice that ate early man's food stores which led to the long relationship between them and us humans, but it is a relationship that evolved far beyond this. The ancient Egyptians mummified dead cats out of respect in the same way as they mummified people, and their goddess, Bastet, was depicted in cat form. The Greeks syncretised their own goddess, Artemis, with Bastet and she too was associated with cats. In turn, in the Middle Ages, Artemis's association with cats was grafted onto the Virgin Mary, with cats included in some beautiful icons of the Annunciation and the Holy Family by artists like Barocci in the sixteenth century.

Here in the twenty-first century, life imitates art with Thomas, aka Mass Cat, as a fitting mascot for the Franciscan Friary. At the end of Mass, with that classic air of feline independence, he nonchalantly wanders off like Yeats's cat Minnaloushe: 'Alone, important and wise.'

For Fear of Little Men ❧

Up the airy mountain,
Down the rushy glen,
We daren't go a-hunting,
For fear of little men;
Wee folk, good folk,
Trooping all together;
Green jacket, red cap,
And white owl's feather.

here are few who do not know by heart, from school days, this first verse of 'The Fairies' by William Allingham; however, I have difficulty understanding why it is such a beloved poem. Perhaps few go on to learn all six stanzas with their unfolding macabre story of these little men or perhaps readers are lulled by the light, tripping metre of the poem, which is so at odds with the doings of these little men.

Some, though, have heard the darkness underneath. The opening lines have been used in settings as diverse as the 1973 horror film *Don't Look in the Basement*, 1971's *Willy Wonka & the Chocolate Factory*, and 'For Fear of Little Men' was the working title of Terry Pratchett's second young adult Discworld novel, which became *The Wee Free Men*.

Even as a child growing up near Ballyshannon, the town from which the poet hails, the poem filled me with a nameless dread, rather than the excited terror that attracts children to the macabre. These were not the gauzy winged, wand-waving fairies from the stories I loved. They were malign, sinister creatures, which not only hunted in gangs, and press-ganged frogs into their evil service, but who also lurked both by the sea and inland.

> Down along the rocky shore
> Some make their home,
> They live on crispy pancakes
> Of yellow tide-foam;
> Some in the reeds
> Of the black mountain-lake,
> With frogs for their watch-dogs,
> All night awake.

What was really disturbing also was the message that no one, not even their king, could control them.

> High on the hill-top
> The old King sits;
> He is now so old and grey
> He's nigh lost his wits.

But it is the fourth stanza, in which little Bridget is stolen, that makes me wonder if there is something in the dark imagination of the poet that foreshadows real-life events, or is it just that when darkness is visited on real life I feel again that frisson of fear I felt when I heard the poem as a child?

> They stole little Bridget
> For seven years long;
> When she came down again
> Her friends were all gone.
>
> They took her lightly back
> Between the night and morrow;
> They thought she was fast asleep,
> But she was dead with sorrow.
>
> They have kept her ever since
> Deep within the lake,
> On a bed of flag-leaves,
> Watching till she wake.

Of course, Allingham was drawing on much older stories from Celtic folklore of fairies and changelings, and another poet from the same area, W.B. Yeats, born forty years after Allingham, echoed this same theme in 'The Stolen Child'.

> Come away, O human child!
> To the waters and the wild
> With a faery, hand in hand,
> For the world's more full of weeping than you can
> understand.

Still, the fate of little Bridget seems too close to the bone, with its dark undertones seeming to be a precursor to real-life tragedies with which we are all too familiar.

The capriciousness of the fairies is evident in the next stanza, in which there is a sudden descent from the tragedy of the child dead with sorrow to the trivial spitefulness of their revenge on anyone who harms their trees.

> By the craggy hill-side,
> Through the mosses bare,
> They have planted thorn-trees
> For pleasure here and there.
>
> Is any man so daring
> As dig them up in spite,
> He shall find their sharpest thorns
> In his bed at night.

The poem ends with the repetition of the opening, superficially catchy lines, before those scary bogeymen trip off the page – none too soon in my opinion. Yet I cannot get away from Allingham and his fairies. From my window

I look out on St Anne's Church in Ballyshannon, in whose graveyard Allingham's ashes were buried in 1889. It is high up overlooking the town on Mullaghnashee – Mullagh na Sídhe, also known as Sídhe Aodh Ruadh, the Fairy Mound of Red Hugh – where it is believed there is an access point to the middle world of the fairies.

Train Stations and Mothers with Sons

here is something lovely about being met at a train station. It is especially lovely for me this time when the train station is London Euston at rush hour and the welcoming young man towering head and shoulders above the crowd is my eldest son, Eoin. It is my first time to visit him since he got his first proper job in London after leaving college. It is not my first time to be in this train station with him, though. The last time was on my pre-baby outing when I was six months pregnant with him. Now he is the one being protective and I am happy to see him.

In the melee of the crush of humanity in Euston I remember him as a nine-year-old in a similar crush in a remote train station in north-west China, when my outings with him had become more far-flung. There he spotted a sign on the door of a comfortable waiting room in the otherwise jam-packed station. The sign said 'Reserved for Soldiers and Mothers with Sons'. He was delighted with his eligibility for this special treatment and bewildered by my refusal to avail of it. He could not know how that chilling combination of mothers, sons and soldiers brought back for me the anxiety I had felt when he was born. His birth coincided with the Gulf War – the first war brought to us live on our TV screens. During night feeds as he suckled and snuffled I, sleep deprived and emotional, was drawn like a moth to the flame to watch red lines of tracer bombs zigzagging across the screen. I wanted to swaddle him in protective love from the crazy world I had brought him into but there was already the evidence of his own strong life force in the surprising strength of his grip as his tiny fingers closed around mine.

I felt the strength of that grip four years later as he clung to my hand at the classroom door and I knew that this new world of school marked the end of my too-brief time as the centre of his universe. My star, as that of all mothers inevitably must, fell out of orbit and he started to make his own way in the world. On that same trip to China, it is his sense of omnipotence I remember as, on the Great Wall, he fully believed that if it could be seen from space then so could he. That sense of invincibility was shaken a few years later when I, cloistered in my office, was unable to protect him from watching over and over again aeroplanes flying into the Twin Towers. I could no longer scoop him in my arms, kiss it better and make everything okay. Instead we sat together and I read his favourite Dr Seuss book *Oh the Places You'll Go!*

In what seemed like the blink of an eye, he decided to follow in my footsteps and go to college in Belfast, that troubled corner of the world in which a tremulous hope had triumphed. It was a very different Belfast to the one of no-go areas I had known in the 1970s. I wanted to show him all the places where the ghost of my younger self still lingered but I didn't; it was time for him to start making his own memories. His memories are of a vibrant city he criss-crossed on his bike, going wherever the music was and where there were others speaking a language foreign to me of capos, Telecasters and preamps. I have watched him graduate from pat-a-cake to Pokémon to poker and me from mama to mum to an exasperated 'MOTHER!'

Now he has taken off his graduation gown, shed the skin of student life and crossed the water to start the next phase of his adult life. In Euston there are no soldiers, just me, the mother, having to run to keep up with the long legs of my son as he strides confidently into his new life and his future.

WINTER

Remembering the Dead ❧

hey say the dead are always with us, but that's not really true. After the first fierce waves of grief subside, the task of living sinks them farther and farther through the layers of clay. They come back when we least expect them, when the texture of a material or the side view of a face resurrects them brilliantly and fleetingly. Then we feel grief again as in its first hour. Our more recently dead are closer to the surfaces of our lives; we can still hear their voices, see them fully as they were in life. But soon, they too slip through the layers of our memory.

I find myself at the old stone church of Toura, on the banks of the Erne, for the ceremony to mark All Souls' Day. Spruced up with flowers for the occasion, the graves encircle the church like a wreath, with a containing boundary hedge of red-hipped hawthorn separating them from the fields of the small farms all around. I join the big crowd outside the church, made up of generations of relatives of the dead buried here. I get a good place with my back against the sun-warmed stone of the porch, with a view down the path and over the surrounding countryside. As the choir opens with a thin, reedy version of 'Sweet Heart of Jesus', I am once again an awed child inside the church, straining to see where the unearthly music is coming from. In front of me today a chair has been provided for a very old, leather-skinned woman wearing a woolly multicoloured ski hat. She joins in the singing with gusto. The elderly canon, who has been here so long he has both baptised and buried some of those being remembered today, calls out the Rosary through an old tinny megaphone. The five sorrowful mysteries echo eerily back from the surrounding townlands of Carranbeg, Corrakeel, Drumbad and Roscor, names repeated over and over on the tombstones around me. As I count the Hail Marys on my fingers, a young woman, balancing a baby on her hip and clutching cellophane-wrapped flowers, runs along the main road and melts into the crowd. During the 'Hail Holy Queen', as we 'poor banished children of Eve, mourning and weeping in this valley of tears' appeal to Mary, an old tractor putters to a stop down on the road and a farmer, cloth cap in hand, dodges his way into the crowd. The Rosary ends, and the hypnotic rise and fall of the 'Pray for us' of the Litany meshes with the revving of the Donegal-to-Dublin express bus as it tries to negotiate its way through the cars parked askew and blocking its path. The canon and the altar servers move slowly among the graves, sprinkling holy water on them and us, creating a Mexican wave of cross-signing. A young girl in front of me, who has been unwavering in her attention, senses the end and hitches up her white fake-fur jacket to adjust the sparkling silver belt on her flared denim jeans. The choir finish with 'Nearer My God to Thee', but for that hour it has been the dead who have been nearer to us. They have had their moment. It is time now for them to return, back down through the topsoil, the humus, the marly, stony or silty clay right down to the bedrock. The sun is fading. The priest's final blessing is drowned out by the fluting thrill of a blackbird's song.

Barry Britton 2023

The Gifted Life ❦

y father had frequently to be rescued from drowning in the weeks before he died. As the cancer ravished him, a great remembered terror shuddered through his body and his mind. It gave his wasted body unnatural strength – he climbed onto chairs, once toppled a wardrobe, and left bruises on our arms as we became the straws he clutched. He was a child again and the waters of Lough Erne were closing over him.

He knew that he was no cat. For him, there would be just this one life, just the one reprieve from death over seventy years earlier. I knew the story of that reprieve so well from his frequent, whiskey-loosened retelling of it. He told the story with his whole body, his arms rising and falling like the water and, at the end, he would give a bemused shake of his head, as though still bewildered by the good fortune of the life he had been gifted.

As death approached, it was this ancient trauma which surfaced through the richly packed sedimented layers of his life. As a young boy growing up on the shores of Lough Erne, he was delighted when two older boys invited him to go out fishing with them. It was his first time in a boat, the magical shift of seeing his familiar world from a different angle, the splash as the oars sliced through the smooth water of the lough, the splish-splosh as the boat sculled away from his father's familiar fertile green fields, which gave way to the yellow wild iris and marsh marigolds fringing the water.

Maybe because the fish weren't biting, maybe because the harshness of their lives had made stones of their hearts, or maybe it was only, as my father reckoned, 'for a bit of sport', the boys threw my father out of the boat. Down, down, down he sank, like a stone, into that unknown world of murky greenness under the water's smooth surface, his lungs bursting with the effort of holding his breath, the water gurgling in when he could no longer do so, and with it his desire to surrender to its insistence. As Emily Dickinson writes:

> Drowning is not so pitiful
> As the attempt to rise
> Three times, 'tis said, a sinking man
> Comes up to face the skies.

He came up once, twice, desperately trying to cling onto the tangle of underwater reeds that gave way under his grasp. It was only when he surfaced for the third time that the boys managed to haul him onto the boat, where he flopped like a dying fish, water streaming from his mouth and nose. The boys carried him, half dead, to his home, where they told his mother he had fallen out of the boat and they had rescued him. In those days, when silence was a child's best protection, he never told his parents the truth of what had happened, but he told us that the men those boys became could never look him in the eye.

He spent all his life on the shores of that same lough, but never again left dry land, and instilled into us, his children, his awareness of that union of what is beautiful with what is terrifying.

Death, defeated that day on the lough, had to skulk around for over seventy years before it was able to claim him. The difference was that in that time, he had accumulated the love of not only his own seven children, but of seven more daughters- and sons-in-law, and a flock of grandchildren. This love formed the bulwark against the rising water coming to claim him. We spread the pages of the *Fermanagh Herald* on the floor and they became for him safe stepping stones to the Noah's Ark refuge of his bed. There, we stayed beside him night and day, and death, when he at last surrendered, was gentle and peaceful. His face, purged of all fear, relaxed and he had the look of someone who had travelled a long, eventful journey but had now arrived safely.

When he drew his last breath, the mirror was covered and the window of his bedroom opened wide, so that his soul could rise unimpeded to a high-ground heaven.

Auntie Gretta

y Auntie Gretta loved rainy days. In the nursing home, where old age and arthritis had tethered her to a high-backed chair, she told us her love of rain stemmed from the early part of her life, in a big, busy Fermanagh farmhouse on the shores of Lough Erne. There, she said, she loved to wake up under the eaves to the sound of rain thudding on the slate roof above her head. A wet day meant an easy – or at least an easier – day, with less outdoors work.

All through my childhood, I'd heard Gretta described as being so strong and hardworking she could do the farm work of any man: heaving milk churns, carting buckets of feed to calves, herding cattle. You might say Gretta was lucky for having been born into a big, prosperous farm, with its large, two-storey, slate-roofed house, at a time when rural life was hard and most farms were small with a thatched cottage. She was unlucky, however, to have been seen as a big-boned, plain girl, with no rush of suitors to give her a home and a life of her own. Gretta's destiny, it appeared, was to be that of an unpaid farmhand who would look after her parents in their old age.

Her hopes had been raised when Paddy Joe from Cashelard, across the border in Donegal, began a weekly courtship, cycling the six miles to her home with a bag of Emerald toffees for her. PJ had already set tongues wagging by building a tiny, one-room, slate-roofed house for himself, so small that, in his own words, 'If anyone comes in the front door they'll have to back out, as there's not enough room to turn around.'

The assumption was that he'd extend the house when he got married. A mountain of toffees was consumed over the years, but the one-room slate house grew no bigger. This sliver of a dream must have faded for Gretta as she reached her forties, an age when, as locals put it, there was 'no risk of a pram in the hallway'. Gretta appeared to have no option but acceptance of her place.

What happened next took on the status of a fairy tale for me as a child. A real-life prince in the unlikely guise of Tony, a retired guard from Buncrana, came to the rescue of my much-loved Auntie Gretta.

She was crossing the border to Ballyshannon on her bicycle one wet day when she got a puncture. This left her stranded in the no-man's land between the northern and southern custom huts, equidistance from her home and her destination. A devoutly religious man, Tony was on his way home from his annual three-day pilgrimage to Lough Derg when, stopping at the customs hut, he spotted the soaked and forlorn Gretta. He went to help, put her bicycle into the boot of the car and gave her a lift to Ballyshannon. Gretta never told us exactly what was said on that journey but evidently by the time they reached Ballyshannon, what should have been an ending had become instead a beginning.

A barely imaginable future unfolded for both of them. As unlikely a couple as they might have seemed to others, they must have seen in each other the potential to meet their deepest longings. I still remember the flurry of disbelief mixed with envy in the family, when, in a very short time and without even a by-your-leave, Gretta was married and queen of her own castle, a neat town house on the main street of Buncrana, as far removed from her isolated rural life as could be imagined. She blossomed in this new life, delighting in having neighbours, shops, a chapel she could walk to and, most magical of all, a beach on her doorstep.

I know all this from when I stayed with her on summer holidays. Sitting together on a bench by the sea, eating 99s, I felt I would burst with happiness. Her home was, to me, coming from a large rambunctious family of seven, truly a palace – spotless with the jewel colours of statues and holy pictures in every room.

Tony was a kind presence who would gently chide Gretta when she wondered if she should let me watch *Top of the Pops* on the black and white TV. 'Let the child enjoy herself,' he'd say. Gretta shared twenty happy years with Tony and lived on in Buncrana after his death until, in her old age, she moved back to a nursing home in Belleek.

She rests now in Buncrana, beside her gentle prince. In Ballyshannon, whenever I walk past the ruins of Paddy Joe's tiny house, where he lived out the rest of his life, eating toffees alone, I think of Gretta and Tony's tranquil happiness in that town house, where the sound of fat raindrops clattering on a roof was no longer needed as a refuge from life.